HOW TO TEACH GROWN-UPS ABOUT CLIMATE CHANGE

HOW TO TEACH GROWN-UPS ABOUT CLIMATE CHANGE

THE CUTTING-EDGE SCIENCE OF OUR CHANGING PLANET

Foreword by **DR. MICHAEL E. MANN**

Written by **PATRICIA DANIELS**

Illustrations by **AARON BLECHA**

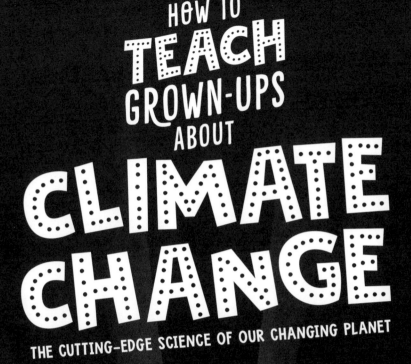

What on Earth Books

Contents

Foreword

As you read *How to Teach Grown-ups About Climate Change*, you're going to find out some amazing things about our planet's past that tell us about today. Did you know, for instance, that Earth has gone through natural warm periods before? For example, during the Jurassic period 200 million years ago, the planet was so warm that dinosaurs roamed even the polar regions. These past warm periods were a consequence of high levels of the planet-warming "greenhouse gas" known as carbon dioxide. Carbon

dioxide levels in Earth's atmosphere rose and fell due to long-term natural cycles that occur over tens of millions of years. Today carbon dioxide levels are rising similar amounts in just decades. That's *a million times faster.* And the cause now is human activities—like driving cars and running power plants. These send fumes from what we call fossil fuels—oil, gas, and coal—into the atmosphere.

Human beings and other living things can adjust to very slow changes in our environment. But dramatic changes that happen quickly pose a far greater threat. Just look around. Today's rapid warming is causing extreme heat, powerful storms, and flooding.

That's the bad news. The good news is that you can help get the planet back on track. Young people like you are speaking out and demanding action of the adults who set the rules. Use this book as a guide to start your own campaign— at home, at school, and in your neighborhood. The battle to preserve our planet has only just begun—and you can lead the way.

Michael E. Mann

Presidential Distinguished Professor and Director of the Center for Science, Sustainability, and the Media, University of Pennsylvania

Are Your Grown-ups Clueless?

Does this sound familiar?

"So what if temperatures go up a degree or two? What's so bad about that?"

Or, "We can't do anything about it now. It's too late to stop it."

Or, "It's time to wade to school. Pull on your tall boots."

Okay, maybe not that last one. Yet.

The point is, if you're like most people, you have grown-ups in your life who are clueless about climate change. But don't worry. This book is a guide to getting the message across to them. You'll discover how you and your grown-ups can work together to help end the climate crisis and heal our warming world.

We Live on the
Best Planet

It's a fact. Our beautiful blue and green planet is the perfect
place for us. Earth circles the Sun at just the right distance to
keep liquid water on the surface. Too far away and the water
would freeze. Too close and it would boil. And living things
on our planet depend on water to keep their bodies working.
Some astronomers call this area around the Sun the
"Goldilocks Zone": just like little bear's porridge in the fairy
tale, it's not too hot and not too cold. It's just right.

More than 8 million kinds of plants and animals grow
and swim and crawl and fly across Earth, including some that
humans haven't yet discovered. Many of them live in Earth's

Sun

TOO HOT

Earth

TOO COLD

JUST RIGHT

ocean, which covers about two-thirds of the world. Ice caps topping the North and South Poles help keep Earth cool and provide a home for our friends the polar bears (in the north) and penguins (in the south).

The atmosphere, our air, warms and shelters us. It even shields us from incoming meteorites (a fact that people don't appreciate as much as they should). Sunlight shining through that air feeds plants and powers winds. Everything on the planet works together in a vast humming web of life and land and water and air and energy. Thanks, Earth!

If Earth could talk, it might say, "You can thank me by cleaning up your act." For more than 200 years, humanity's fuel-burning machines have been giving off gases that change our atmosphere. These gases trap heat in our air, which changes Earth's *climate*—its typical weather over time. That spells trouble. Trouble for us humans, trouble for animals, and trouble for the planet's carefully balanced web of life.

So your adults need to understand that we must deal with this right now. It's a big challenge, but we *can* do it. We have all the tools we need to fix the problems of climate change. And kids are leading the way. Young activists around the world are working together for a better future. After a long struggle just to get people to pay attention, kids have helped to turn the tide. It's time for your grown-ups to join in.

What Does "Climate Change" Mean, Anyway?

Your adults just walked into the house on a brisk winter day. "Brrr! It's freezing out there!" they complain. "So much for global warming!"

Time to give them "The Talk": Weather isn't climate.

Weather, you can explain, is what's happening right now. Maybe it's pelting down rain. Or it's hot enough to fry an egg on the sidewalk. (Who would eat that, anyway? Ugh.) Weather is what you feel on your skin when you step outside.

Holy Humpty!

Climate is different. It's the average of all those weather moments over many years—typically 30 years or so—for any region on Earth. How much rain has fallen, on average, in one spot over the past 30 years? What are the usual temperatures in each season? How much wind, how many sunny days, how much snow has an area felt day after day, year after year? Do the math and you get averages for all these measurements. These are called "climate normals."

Some people say, "Climate is what you expect. Weather is what you get." So tell your grown-ups that the cold winter day is just a cold winter day. That's weather for you. BUT, when the average temperature of that particular day goes up, year after year after year, that's climate change. Climate change does *affect* the weather. Because the planet is warming up, heat waves are lasting longer and storms are getting stronger. Those cold days your grown-ups complained about aren't getting any colder—but the hot days are getting hotter.

Our planet has seen a lot of climate ups and downs in its 4.6-billion-year history. Its atmosphere has evolved, and ice ages have come and gone. But these changes were usually natural and sloooow. They came from little shifts in Earth's orbit, or from cracks opening and closing in Earth's crust, or from new forms of life growing in the ocean.

OUR CLIMATE: A HISTORY

Show your grown-ups that climate changes through time have been both natural and human-made.

700 MILLION YEARS AGO. Ice covers almost all of "Snowball Earth." Simple animals live in the oceans. CLIMATE: Freezing.

2.3 BILLION YEARS AGO. Tiny microbes in Earth's vast ocean start giving off oxygen gas. CLIMATE: Warm, no ice.

92 MILLION YEARS AGO. High levels of carbon dioxide keep the planet extra warm. Dinosaurs roam the land. CLIMATE: Hot and humid.

35 MILLION YEARS AGO.
Carbon dioxide in the air
drops, and Earth cools off.
Ice forms again at the poles.
Big mammals do well.
CLIMATE: Mild, but warmer
than today.

21,500 YEARS AGO. Ice sheets
cover the planet as far
south as present-day New
York City. Humans live side
by side with mammoths and
sabre-toothed cats.
CLIMATE: Icy and much
colder than today.

TODAY.
The poles are still icy,
but melting. Carbon
dioxide levels are rising
sharply. Humans and
their machines
dominate the planet.
CLIMATE: Changing
quickly from cool to
warm and steamy.

The changes we're talking about now *aren't* natural. They're *not* slow. Because of human activity, temperatures on Earth have shot up, especially in the past 70 years or so. Overall, the planet is toastier now than it has been for thousands of years. We used to call this whole process "global warming," but "climate change" is a better description. When the atmosphere traps more heat, it doesn't just give you that icky sweaty feeling. It melts ice sheets, supercharges storms, strengthens floods and droughts, and reshapes our whole environment.

IT'S A FACT

In June 2020, the Siberian town of Verkhoyansk, Russia, reached 100.4°F (38°C). It was the hottest temperature ever recorded north of the Arctic Circle.

But this is just one theory. Climate scientists are still debating this, right?

NOPE!

You can correct your grown-up immediately if they make this argument.

Climate change, driven by humans, is a scientific fact. It's as real as gravity, or radio waves, or tomorrow's homework. More than 99 percent of climate scientists around the world agree. As one scientist puts it:

It's warming.

It's us.

We're sure.

It's bad.

We can fix it.

In fact, we MUST fix it.

How Did We Get Here?

You can help your grown-ups understand the whole climate thing by first explaining how the atmosphere works.

The atmosphere seems huge from the ground, but in fact it is a thin, thin blanket of air and clouds clinging to Earth's surface. It's made mostly of two gases: nitrogen and oxygen. It also holds small amounts of other gases, such as water vapor (water in the form of a gas, kind of like steam), carbon dioxide, methane, and nitrous oxide.

Other stuff floats around in the air, too, such as dust, salt, ash, and smoke.

Nitrogen and oxygen are basically "invisible" to heat. Heat from the Sun passes right through them and warms the land and ocean. Heat from the land and ocean rises up and sails through these gases into space. It's the other gases that come into play with climate change. We call them "greenhouse gases."

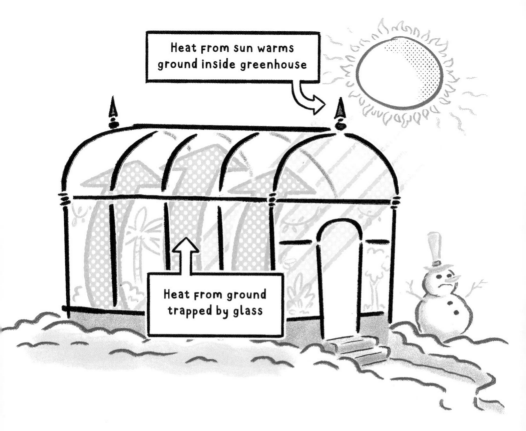

Heat from sun warms ground inside greenhouse

Heat from ground trapped by glass

Greenhouse gases, such as carbon dioxide (CO_2), methane, or nitrous oxide, don't let all the heat escape into space. They keep some of it trapped in the atmosphere, warming Earth—a little like the way the glass of a greenhouse traps heat inside. If we didn't have greenhouse gases, our planet would be much colder.

So why are greenhouse gases so bad? ask your puzzled grown-ups. They aren't, you tell them. Not when they're left alone, as they were until 1750 or so. Around then, humans started to add more of these gases to the atmosphere and threw off the whole delicate balance of sunlight and air.

Fossils in the Air

Remember when you had to ride your horse to town? When you had to blow out your candles and go to bed in the cold? Me neither. But these were facts of life for almost everyone in the world until the 19th century. In the late 18th century, the big upheaval we now call the Industrial Revolution began. Starting in Britain, and spreading around the world, people began to use machines to do work that they used to toil over by hand. As the years went by, engines began to power factories and propel "horseless carriages"—what we now call cars. Electricity lit up cities. Airplanes took to the skies.

Machines changed farming, too. Farms got bigger when they had machines to do the heavy labor. Chemicals made in labs helped plants and animals grow fatter, faster.

The engines behind the Industrial Revolution were fed by fossil fuels. No, not big fossils, like *T. rex* jaws or stegosaur thigh bones. Fossil fuels come from tiny plants and single-celled

WHAT YOU CAN DO

Ask your grown-ups if they truly need to drive an energy-eating car on their next trip out of the house. Could they walk instead? Ride a bicycle? It would be good for their health as well as the planet's.

Fossil fuels come from plants and tiny animals buried long ago.

animals that lived long ago. These prehistoric life-forms stored energy from the Sun in their bodies to make carbon and hydrogen. Trees are a little like straws that suck out CO_2 from the air to make their trunks and branches. When they die, the tiny plants' itty-bitty bodies and all that wood from the trees are buried and squeezed and heated underground. They change into the substances we know today as fossil fuels: mainly coal (that's the trees), natural gas, and oil (the remains of ancient creatures). When people realized these materials could be used for fuel, they started digging them up and setting them on fire.

In the years since the Industrial Revolution, factories and cities and roads and giant farms have spread worldwide. Earth's population has grown from a billion people in 1800 to over 8 billion today. And almost all

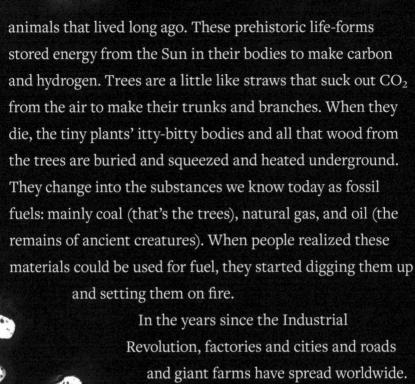

of us are enthusiastically torching fossil fuels to keep our machines running.

So here's the problem, you tell your grown-ups. We can't dig up, move, or burn fossil fuels cleanly. Some of the carbon stored in those trees and teeny bodies long ago zooms back into the atmosphere—mainly as carbon dioxide, but also as methane, nitrous oxide, and other greenhouse gases. Carbon dioxide has been building up in the air since the Industrial Revolution.

Scientists today measure carbon dioxide in the atmosphere in parts per million, or ppm. (Parts of *what* per million *who?* Particles of carbon dioxide per million particles of air.) Before the Industrial Revolution, carbon dioxide hovered around 280 ppm. Today, it has reached 421 ppm. This is the most carbon dioxide we've had in the atmosphere in human history.

This is not good.

How Do We Know All This?

"This climate change science is still new, though, isn't it?" asks your well-meaning grown-up. "I mean, we only started studying it a few years ago."

No, indeed. People have known about the link between carbon and warming temperatures for more than 150 years.

In the 1850s, for instance, American scientist Eunice Newton Foote turned from her quest to get women the vote to experiments with carbon dioxide. She compared the temperatures of gases inside different glass containers placed in the sunlight, finding that the ones holding carbon dioxide gas heated up more and cooled down more slowly than the others. "An atmosphere of that gas would give to our Earth a high temperature," she noted in an 1856 paper.

Soon afterward, Irish physicist and avid mountain climber John Tyndall ran experiments showing that not only carbon dioxide but also other gases warmed Earth. For instance, "without water vapor," he noted, the land would be "held fast in the iron grip of frost."

Then there's Svante Arrhenius, a Swedish chemist from later in the 1800s. He was a smart guy with loads of curiosity, a mind for math, and an excellent bushy mustache. In the 1890s, Arrhenius began to study ice ages, the regular cooling

Svante
Arrhenius

periods in Earth's history. He collected measurements for
temperatures and humidity from around the world and for a
solid year, he and his mustache sat at his desk and worked out
tens of thousands of calculations in pencil.

Even Arrhenius said this work was "tedious." But the
math was clear. Carbon dioxide helps to trap heat in the air.
When you add more of it, temperatures go up, like heat
trapped in a greenhouse. Arrhenius called it the "hothouse
theory." At the time he wasn't too worried about this.

Arrhenius lived in Sweden. It's cold there. He thought a little warming would be nice.

Your grown-ups lighten up. Maybe that's true. Maybe the chilly north would like to be a bit milder? Maybe the glaciers would like to melt?

Wrong again. About 120 years later, another Swede, a descendant of Arrhenius himself, is helping the world understand that warming is definitely *not* so nice. Her name is Greta Thunberg, and she's been an activist since she was 15 years old. Get ready to tell your grown-ups about her on page 82.

A bit more heat might be nice!

HOW WE KNOW IT'S HOT

Tens of thousands of weather detectors on land and sea, and in the air and space, measure the world's weather every day.

In the air, weather balloons detect temperatures, pressure, and moisture. Passenger planes also collect weather information as they fly.

Weather stations on land track temperatures, rain and snow, wind speed, and more.

In space, satellites measure gases in the atmosphere and spot changes in ice cover and sea levels.

At sea, buoys and ships measure air and water temperatures, wind speed, waves, and more.

Ice Cores, Tree Rings, and Satellites

Today's scientists are *so* grateful they have computers to help them sort through the mountains of evidence for climate change. With modern methods, they have been able to track temperatures and gases back thousands of years. For instance, some researchers bundle up in their warmest coats to drill into the world's ice sheets. There, they pull out long cylinders of ice that hold air samples nearly 3 million years old.

Mammoths could have breathed that air! Scientists also track temperature and climate history in old weather station records, tree rings, coral reefs, and sediment that sits on the bottom of the ocean.

You know Eunice or Arrhenius would have loved to see our planet from outer space. We can do that now with spacecraft orbiting Earth. More than 160 climate satellites keep their electronic eyes on our land, ocean, air, and ice. They can even detect melting ice by measuring tiny changes in Earth's gravity.

Mis-, Dis-, and Information

By now, you can see that your grown-ups may have picked up some odd (ahem... *wrong*) ideas about climate change. This is common. You can teach them how to find information they can trust, while avoiding misinformation (false or misleading info) and disinformation (*deliberately* false or misleading info).

Much of the bogus news about climate change spreads on social media. Then it multiplies as people share it with their friends, creating what information experts call an "echo chamber." Common arguments your grown-ups might see are:

It's not really happening.

It's not an emergency.

That climate scientist is a big phony.

Tell your grown-ups to be skeptical when they see such messages, especially online. They need to ask, Who made this message? Who paid for it? What do they get out of it?

Your grown-ups can and should double-check any suspicious messages against recognized scientific authorities, trustworthy news sites, respectable encyclopedias and other references, and websites that debunk fake information. (See the Further Reading section on page 98.)

Where Does It All Come From?

Today, most greenhouse gases arise from a few areas of modern life: making electricity for businesses and homes, growing food (both plants and animals), and moving ourselves and our belongings in cars, trucks, ships, and airplanes. We get most of the energy for these activities by burning oil, coal, and natural gas. And when fossil fuels burn in our engines and power plants, the carbon they hold combines with oxygen to make carbon dioxide gas. This greenhouse gas then floats into the air.

Do your grown-ups like pies? Show them this one: It's a pie chart showing where greenhouses gases such as carbon dioxide and methane come from. The size of each slice shows the relative amount of greenhouse gases each source gives off.

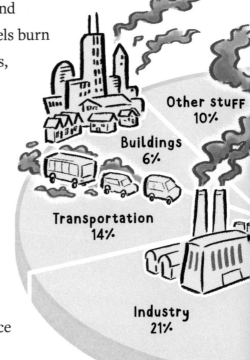

Other stuff 10%

Buildings 6%

Transportation 14%

Industry 21%

SOURCES OF GREENHOUSE GASES

Yuck! I know one big source of methane: cow farts!

NOPE!

Well, okay, partial credit. Cow farts do add a little bit of methane to the air. But it's cow burps that really gas up the joint. Cows have four-part stomachs that work hard to digest plants. This digestion process gives off a lot of methane gas, which the cows belch out without even saying, "Excuse moo." One cow can produce 220 pounds (100 kg) of methane each year. Multiply that by one billion—the number of cows in the world—and that's a heck of a lot of gas.

Methane itself doesn't smell bad. Unfortunately, it's a powerful greenhouse gas. It doesn't last as long in the air as carbon dioxide, but it's much better at trapping heat.

Electricity production 25%

Farming 24%

Tell your grown-ups that if they're really interested in evil greenhouse farts, they should look at dinosaurs. Scientists have researched whether plant-eating dinosaurs might have tooted out enough methane to warm up the Jurassic period. More study is needed, but it certainly looks possible.

So who are all these wasteful people, driving around and raising cows? They are us. Every human uses food and energy. In worldwide terms, the richest countries and the ones with the most people add the most greenhouse gases to the air. For instance, China, the United States, and India give off billions of tons of these gases each year. If you measure greenhouse gases per person, then Canada, the United States, Australia, and Saudi Arabia are among the main culprits.

You can also map out greenhouse gases per company. More than two-thirds of the greenhouse gases that have warmed the planet's air in recent years come from about 100 fossil fuel companies. Remind your grown-ups that they can put pressure on these companies, and the governments that support them, to change their ways.

At the same time that we're pumping so much greenhouse gas into the air, we're getting rid of one of our best ways to soak it up: forests. Trees live on carbon dioxide. They pull it in from the air to feed themselves. But people in many countries, particularly in tropical places, are cutting down forests to make room for farms and cattle ranches, mines and roads. We're losing natural allies in the fight against climate change.

Leaves use energy from the Sun to change carbon dioxide and water into sugar, the plant's food.

Leaves take in carbon dixoide from the air.

Leaves release leftover oxygen into the air.

Roots pull in water.

Climate change is totally unfair. Some of the countries that add the smallest amounts of greenhouse gases are feeling the biggest impacts. Poor people use less energy than rich people but suffer more from these climate changes. Folks in low-income countries are much more likely to make a living from the land and water by farming and fishing. When droughts and floods occur, they don't have enough money to move somewhere else or to build expensive structures to protect themselves. Many of these people live in hotter parts of the world to begin with. They are more likely to suffer from deadly heat waves. Remind your grown-ups that when they do their bit to fight climate change, they're fighting for everyone on the planet.

IT'S A FACT!

Congratulations to the small nation of Suriname. Thanks in part to their widespread forests, they have already reached "net-zero" greenhouse gas emissions. That means they take as much greenhouse gas out of the atmosphere as they put in.

The Hockey Stick

So now you've told your grown-ups about greenhouse gases
and where they come from. It's time to explain what they do
to the world.

In 1999, climate scientist Michael Mann published a
scientific study about world temperatures over the previous
1,000 years. A graph in the paper showed that temperatures
stayed about the same until around the year 1900. Then they
shot steeply upward.

Dr. Mann didn't call his graph a hockey stick, but other
people soon did, because that's what it looked like—a hockey
stick on its back, with its blade sticking up. Climate deniers
have attacked the hockey stick picture of global warming ever
since it was published.

GOING UP!

In the 20th century, big increases in carbon dioxide made world temperatures shoot up. A graph of the sudden temperature rise looks like a hockey stick.

For almost 1,000 years, temperatures were pretty steady.

CHANGE IN TEMP IN °C

0.5

0.0

-0.5

-1.0

YEAR ▶ 1100   1200   1300   1400   1500

However, scientists have shown over and over again that it's right. And temperatures are still rising.

Your grown-up peers at the graph and points out something: Temperatures have gone up, sure, but only by a little more than 1°C (1.8°F) so far. That's not so much, right?

Not for us humans. But it's a big deal for Earth. Our planet is highly sensitive to worldwide temperature changes. A steady rise in heat messes up Earth's balanced web of air and water and ice and land and life. Just how bad the effects will be depends on us. We need to clamp down on climbing temperatures. We need to flatten the hockey blade.

It's too late... sigh...
I heard that temperatures
will keep climbing for 30
or 40 years, no matter
what we do.

NOPE!

If we quit adding carbon dioxide to the air today, temperatures will stop rising within a few years. Your grown-ups are remembering old news, which said that carbon lasts for so long in the atmosphere that it would keep trapping heat for decades. Now scientists know that the ocean and forests soak up much of this extra carbon. If we stop giving off carbon gases, temperatures will level off quickly. The atmosphere won't cool down, though. It is already warm enough that some climate change effects, such as melting sea ice, will keep going no matter what. But we could avoid the increasingly bad results that would come with climbing temperatures.

That's good news!

If we cut our greenhouse gas outflows sharply in the next few years, we could keep the increase in world temperatures to around 3.2°F (1.8°C) by the year 2100. If we cut gases just a little, temperatures will go up by about 3.6°F to 6.3°F (2°C to 3.5°C). If we keep adding to the gases, Earth will heat up by 5.9 to 10.3°F (3.3°C to 5.7°C). The higher the temperatures, the more damage they do to the planet.

Rising temperatures change so many things in so many surprising ways that sometimes we call their effects "global weirding" instead of the old term, *global warming*. Sit your grown-ups down. It's time to explain just what to expect.

Global Weirding

The first thing your adults need to know is that climate change is already here. All of the weirdness you're going to tell them about has already begun. Just how bad it will get in the years to come is up to us.

Let's start with one of the most obvious effects of rising heat: even more heat. The world's hottest places are getting hotter. Heat waves—long periods of unusually hot weather—are happening more often, lasting longer, and getting more intense. Meanwhile, record periods of cold weather (nobody calls them cold waves) are getting fewer and fewer. In 2021, the normally cool Northwest United States and nearby Canada zoomed above 117°F (47°C) in the summer. Snails there were cooked alive in their shells. Death Valley, California, set an unofficial record of 130°F (54.4°C) the same year.

The world's coldest places are also getting hotter. On a single day in 2022, temperatures in the Arctic were 50°F (28°C) warmer than average, while they were 70°F (39°C) warmer than average in Antarctica. Scientists there posed for pictures in their shorts.

Cities, in particular, are "heat islands." All those buildings and roads soak up the heat during the day and stay hot at night. Not only is this heat dangerous to everyone's health, it also boosts energy use as people crank up their air-conditioning. That's if you have air-conditioning. Many people in the hottest places do not.

Hot air dries out trees and other plants, which leads to another climate change effect: wildfires. Spread by hot dry winds through forests and grasslands, these kinds of fires are increasing. In 2019 and 2020, wildfires in Australia torched millions of acres (hectares) of land. The fires killed or displaced billions of animals— including some of Australia's most famous and already endangered critters, such as koalas and wombats. Wildfires are setting more plants ablaze not only in places that are used to fires, such as Australia or California, but even in the chilly Arctic.

Hot plus dry adds up to drought. Climate change is bringing long, dry periods that shrink rivers and lakes. In recent years, countries in Europe have been hit by the worst droughts in 2,000 years, since Roman soldiers roamed the land. In India, thirsty farms have drained so

WHAT YOU CAN DO

Shade trees—big trees that spread out at their tops— eat carbon and cool cities. Encourage your grown-ups to plant a tree in their yard or neighborhood. If you live in a city, find out if your city is one of the official Tree Cities of the World. If it's not, you and your grown-ups can get it started. (See Further Reading on page 98.)

much water from the ground that the change can be seen by satellites 300 miles (483 km) above Earth.

And then we have weather. Stormy weather, that is. Crazy intense weather. Heat in the ocean and air powers big storms such as hurricanes. The warmer the air, the more oomph it gives to storms and the more rain the clouds can hold. The planet is already seeing stronger tropical storms, which are dumping heavier rain on us than ever before. Ask people in Texas about Hurricane Harvey. In 2017, it poured well over four feet (more than a meter) of rain onto the city of Houston. Cars floated away. Highways turned into rivers. People caught fish in their living rooms. Scientists say that climate change made Harvey much stronger than it would have been otherwise. They also say that the world will see more superstorms like Harvey in the future.

We're in Hot Water

Maybe all this talk of fire and drought has your grown-ups thinking fondly of the cool, refreshing ocean. No wildfires there!

No... but in many ways, you'll have to inform them, climate change hurts the ocean most of all. Sorry.

Tell your adults to think of the ocean as a big sponge. Yes, that's weird, but keep going. The ocean (which covers most of Earth, remember) is great at soaking things up. That includes heat. The ocean drinks in heat from the Sun and air during the day and releases it slowly at night. That's why Earth's temperatures don't zoom way up and down from day to night. As air temperatures rise due to climate change, the ocean warms up, too. It is now the hottest it has been since we started keeping track in the 19th century.

Our ocean sponge is also excellent at soaking up carbon dioxide from the air. When carbon dissolves in seawater, it changes the water's chemistry, making it a lot more acidic. It hurts ocean animals that can't survive in acid-y waters—especially coral animals. Heat and acidity are killing coral reefs

WHAT YOU CAN DO

Replace your old-style light bulbs with LED (light-emitting diode) bulbs. For each bulb you change, you'll save hundreds of pounds (kilograms) of carbon from being pumped into the air.

around the world. These colorful, lacy structures, some of them thousands of years old, are turning dead white. All kinds of ocean creatures are losing their coral homes.

The ocean is made of salt water, of course, but the ocean lives next to, or sometimes underneath, a whole lot of fresh water ice. (Salt water, no surprise here, holds dissolved salt. It is denser and heavier than fresh water. Rain and lakes and rivers and ice are made of fresh water.) Around the North Pole, giant slabs of ice cover the Arctic Ocean. Ice sheets hug the continent of Antarctica. Great slow-moving rivers of ice, called glaciers, gleam in mountains and valleys around the planet.

Ask your grown-ups: What happens when you heat ice? That's right—it melts. Warmer air and the warmer ocean are melting our sea ice and glaciers. Arctic sea ice has been thinning and melting away for at least 40 years. Ice shelves around Antarctica are breaking up. Ice sheets on the cold island of Greenland are turning into water and running into the sea. More than a trillion tons of ice a year are vanishing.

Uh oh! All that melting Arctic sea ice is going to raise our sea levels.

NOPE!

Floating Arctic sea ice is already taking up room in the ocean. When it melts, it goes from solid to liquid, but it takes up about the same amount of space. However, Arctic ice that melts on land and runs into the ocean is different. Ice sheets and glaciers on the big island of Greenland, on mountains around the world, and around some parts of Antarctica are turning to water and running off into the sea. It wasn't in the ocean before, so every drop of water from melting ice on land raises the sea level.

We're full! Go back!

NO VACANCY

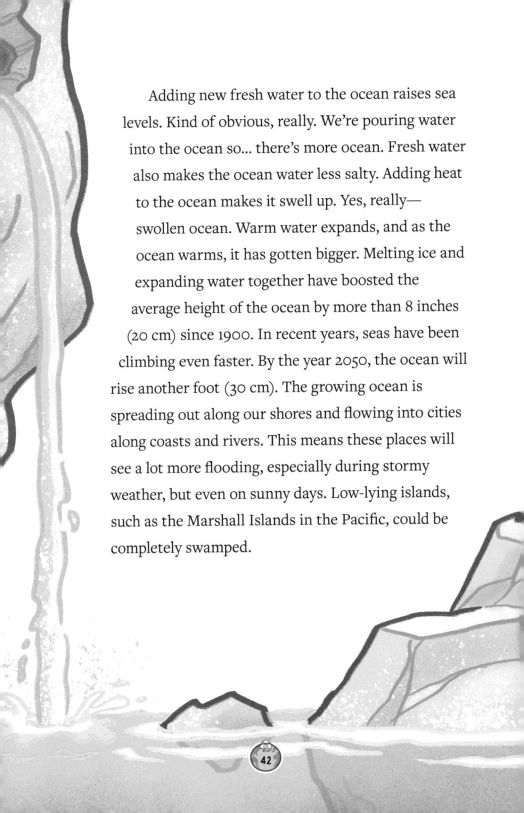

Adding new fresh water to the ocean raises sea levels. Kind of obvious, really. We're pouring water into the ocean so... there's more ocean. Fresh water also makes the ocean water less salty. Adding heat to the ocean makes it swell up. Yes, really— swollen ocean. Warm water expands, and as the ocean warms, it has gotten bigger. Melting ice and expanding water together have boosted the average height of the ocean by more than 8 inches (20 cm) since 1900. In recent years, seas have been climbing even faster. By the year 2050, the ocean will rise another foot (30 cm). The growing ocean is spreading out along our shores and flowing into cities along coasts and rivers. This means these places will see a lot more flooding, especially during stormy weather, but even on sunny days. Low-lying islands, such as the Marshall Islands in the Pacific, could be completely swamped.

IT'S A FACT!

To protect themselves against rising waters, the people of Jakarta, Indonesia, are building a giant seawall in the shape of Garuda, a huge mythical bird.

Floods hurt plants and animals as well as people. Animals lose their homes to floodwaters. Most trees, needing fresh water, can't grow in salty places.

And if all that doesn't wake up your grown-ups, drop this little bomb on them: They could lose their internet. Many cables are buried near the shore. They aren't made to take a saltwater bath.

People and Other Animals

All of us animals, from the tiniest fly to the heftiest elephant, have to live on this changing Earth. Many of us will have a hard time adjusting.

Even your most out-of-touch grown-ups probably know climate change's most famous animal, global warming's VIP: the polar bear. Polar bears make their living on Arctic sea ice. They hunt there, travel there, and sleep there. With Arctic ice rapidly melting, polar bears are in big trouble.

They aren't the only ones. All animals are adapted to their own habitats. Each has a natural neighborhood with its own special food and shelter. Warming temperatures, floods in some places, droughts in others, melting ice, wildfires, and all the other nasty effects of global weirding change these habitats. Ocean creatures, for instance, are really feeling the heat. The ocean isn't just warming and getting more acidic—ocean waters are also losing the oxygen that many plants and animals need for survival.

Some animals will adapt. Others can't. Many creatures are already on the move, both in the ocean and on land. They're traveling toward the poles or up mountains, where the weather is cooler. Europe's purple emperor butterflies moved their range north by 125 miles (201 km) in just 10 years. Moose are clomping around on new ground in Alaska and Canada. Mosquitoes are carrying diseases to places where they've never been felt before. Adaptable plants are taking root farther north or south, or farther uphill, or blooming earlier. Where they can't adapt, they're dying out. "Those poor animals," say your grown-ups.

WORLD CLIMATE CHANGE TOUR

Take your grown-ups on a little world tour,
a nature-watching expedition.

EUROPE:

In Germany, hotter air lures bark beetles into spruce forests. These little insects and drier weather are killing off the tall trees.

NORTH AMERICA:

Snowshoe hares turn white every winter, which helps them blend in with the snow and hide from enemies. But what if there's no snow? Now the bunnies show up against a brown landscape, bright white targets for predators.

SOUTH AMERICA:

Many birds in the Amazon rainforest are changing shape over time. Their bodies are getting smaller and their wings are getting longer. These changes may help them stay cool as forests get warmer and drier.

EVERYWHERE:

Rising waters are covering beaches, blocking sea turtles from laying their eggs.

ARCTIC:

As sea ice melts, orcas (killer whales) are moving north to hunt in the open waters. This is risky for the orcas, and not so much fun for the bowhead whales they eat.

ASIA:

Sea snot! Yes, sea snot, slimy ooze made from tiny marine animal bodies, has been choking harbors in Turkey's Sea of Marmara. It likes the warmer waters that come with climate change.

AFRICA:

Climate change is killing off trees that African forest elephants like to eat. It's also shrinking the habitat that shelters them. These big creatures are endangered.

AUSTRALIA:

Say goodbye to the Bramble Cay melomys, a furry little rodent. Rising ocean waters have drowned its small island. The melomys has vanished, one of the first mammals to become extinct due to climate change.

WHAT YOU CAN DO

Ask your adults to stop idling—their cars, that is. Gas-powered cars that are parked but still running are just coughing up carbon. If your school has buses idling outside, maybe you and your grown-ups can talk to the school about that, too.

"Aren't you glad you're a modern human, safe in your own home?"

Well, yes and no, you have to tell them. Just like our furry and scaly friends, we depend on our natural surroundings for life. As storms, droughts, and floods increase around the world, millions and millions of people are on the move. These climate migrants can't farm their drying land anymore, or fish in waters too hot for fish. They can't live in blistering heat. Unless your adults take action now, many more families will have to pack up and leave their homes.

Aaaaaaaaaah! It's the end of the world!

NOPE!

Climate change is a crisis, but it's not the end of the world. Not even close. Our sturdy planet has survived for billions of years and will go on for billions more. It has seen life-forms come and go and adapt and evolve. Even if we did nothing about climate change—WHICH IS NOT AN OPTION, DON'T EVEN THINK ABOUT IT—humans would face serious trouble and disruption, but we would struggle along and survive. But why would we want to, when we can fix things right now? When we can make a better world? Tell your grown-ups that predicting doom is just another form of climate denial: It stops us from taking action. Don't do it.

How to Fix It

Oh, your poor grown-ups. They're upset. "This is such a big problem," they moan. "What can we do to stop it?"

We're glad you asked! you say. Yes, it seems overwhelming, but you can do so **MANY, MANY, MANY, MANY, MANY, MANY, MANY, MANY, MANY, MANY, MANY, MANY, MANY, MANY** things right now to save the planet. In fact, people everywhere are already working on this and making good progress. It's time to walk your adults through a world of answers to climate change.

To start, you'll need to make it clear that they can tackle the problem in two ways—and they should choose both. The first way is through personal choices. Your adults can make small but important changes in their own habits and households. If they encourage their friends and family to make changes too, these little fixes add up to big improvements in society as a whole.

The second way to fight the weirding is to start from the top and change the system. When governments and businesses make climate-friendly decisions, they have a gigantic impact right away. So tell your grown-ups, You vote, right? You buy things. Use that power for good!

Turn Off the Water

How do we fight climate change? We stop adding greenhouse gases to the air.

How do we do that? We stop burning fossil fuels. We turn to renewable energy.

Okay? Is that clear?

If not, help your grown-ups imagine it like this. The atmosphere is like a bathtub in a room above us, and it's filling up with water. Soon it's overflowing. We can:

1. Do nothing and let the water gush through the ceiling onto our heads.

2. Run upstairs and scoop the bathwater, cup by cup, into the sink, while the tub continues to overflow.

52

3. Turn the faucet down to a trickle. The tub still overflows, just more slowly.

4. Turn off the faucet. The tub stops running over.

5. Turn off the faucet and open the drain. The tub empties. (But somebody still has to mop up the mess.)

Greenhouse gases, in case your adults don't quite follow, are the water flowing into Earth's atmospheric bathtub. We have to turn off these gases at the source. Then we have to drain them from the atmosphere with better use of our land.

Right now, fossil fuels such as oil, coal, and natural gas give us most of our energy, and as we saw in our yucky pie chart on pages 26–27, those fuels feed carbon dioxide into the air. We need to replace these dirty fuels with clean, renewable energy sources. Your grown-ups ask, What does "renewable" mean exactly? It means the energy comes from natural sources that can't be used up, such as wind or sunlight, which also don't emit carbon dioxide. And no, these kinds of energy are not expensive, and they are not experimental. Solar and wind power are now cheaper to produce than fossil fuels. Turning to these well-established energy sources if they are available near you will save us billions of dollars in the long run.

Maybe your grown-ups have heard the term *carbon footprint*. This is a measurement of the carbon you send into the air through your daily actions. Some websites have calculators that let you see the size of this dirty mark by adding together your travel, household energy, and shopping choices. Small choices add up. Everything we buy has taken energy to produce. When you stop buying things you don't need, when you use less packaging, and when you buy from local producers, you shrink your carbon footprint. But remember: It's not just individual people who have these footprints. Companies and governments also have carbon footprints, and theirs can be gigantic: Godzilla-size prints versus your own mouse-size tracks. Don't let them tell you that it's just up to you to solve climate change. Let them know that you'll be voting for climate-friendly politicians as soon as you're old enough.

WHAT YOU CAN DO

Give your old stuff a second life. Find out where you can recycle items, such as electronics, that you can't add to your recycling bin. Used clothing in good shape can go to secondhand stores. And there you can buy other used clothing, instead of new, which saves both money and carbon! When we waste less, we save energy.

The world is already cleaning up one of the biggest parts of everyone's carbon footprint: cars, trucks, and other transportation. Although electric cars have been around since the 19th century, it wasn't until the 1990s that carmakers started building the kinds of hybrid and electric cars we see today. Hybrid cars run on a combination of battery power and regular gasoline. Electric cars run just on a battery, which is rechargeable— you plug it in when it runs down. Electric cars are light and simple and peppy and don't cough up any greenhouse gases. They do take their power from electricity, which comes from power plants, but overall they are still responsible for much less carbon dioxide than regular cars. That's especially true if local power plants draw on renewable energy in the first place.

More and more people are buying these clean green cars, trucks, and buses. Take a look at Norway. The Land of the Midnight Sun has made buying electric cars cheaper than gasoline cars, so now almost all cars sold there are electric or rechargeable hybrids. Other countries, including the United States, are following their lead in helping folks buy clean green machines.

If most of us are driving electric cars and trucks by the year 2050—or, more likely, if those vehicles are driving themselves and we're just sitting in the back staring out the window—we will have cut our greenhouse gases from transportation by at least two-thirds.

Now turn your grown-ups' attention away from their cool electric cars. What about electricity in general? What's the best way to power up our houses and factories?

IT'S A FACT!

In 1971, people weren't driving electric cars on Earth, but astronauts drove one (a lunar rover) on the Moon.

Windy Sunny Weather Wonders

Let's start with wind. You and your adults have probably seen tall, sci-fi-looking windmills standing on mountain slopes or rising above fields, their white blades sweeping through the air. They can also be spotted out to sea, with their feet buried in the seafloor but their blades high above the waves. Most of us probably haven't seen one up close. They are seriously huge. A typical wind turbine (as they are properly called) is as tall as a 20-story skyscraper. The biggest have blades longer than a football field. These blades can swing around as fast as

IT'S A FACT!

People on the Danish island of Samsø came together to pay for their own wind turbines. Now, the island has net-zero carbon emissions. They make so much clean electricity that they sell some of it back to the mainland.

a speeding race car. Wind turbines are excellent sources of energy. Just one rotation, one round sweep, of a big blade can power a house for a day.

With machines like these, wind power is one of our best sources of renewable energy. "What happens on a calm day?" ask your adults. Well, wind turbines are connected to the larger power grid. When they can't supply power, other sources take over. "What about birds, flying into the blades?" they wonder. That does happen sometimes. But windmill companies are working to avoid bird migration routes and design safer turbines. Environmental groups that support birds, such as the National Audubon Society, are all in favor of properly placed wind power.

STATUE OF LIBERTY
305 Feet (93 m) tall

WIND TURBINE
492 Feet (150 m) tall

But...I heard that UFOs are knocking down wind turbines. Shouldn't we be worried about flying saucer crashes?

NOPE!

People really have said this. In 2009, workers found a blade broken off a turbine in England. The whole machine was wrecked. Bright lights were seen in the sky the night before. Adding two and two together and getting 1,000, some folks decided a low-flying UFO had run into the windmill. Wind turbine experts poured cold water on this theory, explaining that it was a normal accident due to ordinary wear and tear. Remind your grown-ups: Any aliens who can steer between the planets are probably smart enough to avoid a single windmill.

Today, more than 5 percent of the world's electricity comes from wind power, and that percentage will probably grow quickly.

Heat from the Sun, our never-failing source of energy, drives winds that turn windmill blades. We can also use that sunlight directly to power our houses and businesses. Solar power is one of the best known and cheapest forms of renewable energy.

In 1954, scientists focused light on a little panel of silicon (a common element in Earth's crust), and in turn that panel spun a toy Ferris wheel. This was the first practical solar cell. Since then, solar cells have given clean energy to everything from the International Space Station to farms in Australia.

HOW SOLAR PANELS WORK

Solar panels turn the energy in sunlight into electrical energy.

Every solar panel is made of dozens of solar cells.

Each cell is typically made of layers of silicon, covered by glass.

When sunlight hits the silicon, it knocks off little particles called electrons to create an electrical current.

The current travels through the wiring in the panels to send power to a building or a power station.

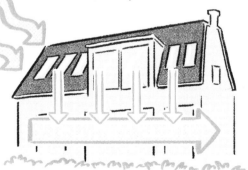

HOW WIND TURBINES WORK

Wind turbines turn wind energy into electrical energy.

Wind makes the blades spin.

Spinning blades turn shafts inside the turbine's nacelle (the big box at the top).

Shafts turn gears, which drive a generator.

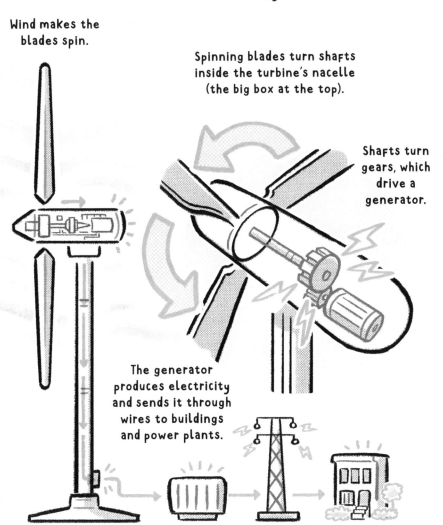

The generator produces electricity and sends it through wires to buildings and power plants.

Solar cells turn sunlight into electricity. They send that electricity out through wires, or store it in a battery, or use it to heat water. They can be as small as the little cells on a calculator or, grouped into panels, they can cover an enormous grassy meadow. On solar farms, row upon row of shiny gray slabs soak up the light, turning like sunflowers to face the Sun as it moves across the sky. These farms feed electricity directly into the grid that supplies communities.

IT'S A FACT!

Using darker and lighter solar panels, China built a big solar farm in the shape of a panda.

Solar panels are practical in small places, too. They fit on roofs and in backyards. They're handy in countries where electricity isn't widespread—just pop some panels on your roof and you can heat your house or watch the latest TV show.

"That's all very well for sunny places during the day," say your grown-ups. "But it's not practical in cloudy countries, is it? And what happens at night? Does our electricity just switch off, leaving us in the dark?"

Let's reassure those worried folks. Help them understand that sunlight is still sunlight on cloudy days. Solar panels work under the clouds, though they don't make as much power as they do in bright sunlight. Not so sunny places like the United Kingdom and Germany harvest plenty of solar power. Batteries can store some solar power to release at night. People are now working on making better batteries for more storage to help that along. And like most renewable energy, solar power is usually tied into an electrical grid that draws on many sources. When one source fades out, another jumps in.

Water and Waste

People have long known that moving water packs a punch. Waterwheels, turning in rushing rivers, have ground our grain for thousands of years. Engines in big dams spin out electrical power without spitting out greenhouse gases. Hydropower, as this is called, is one of the major sources of renewable energy in the world right now.

But hydropower from big dams is not great for the environment in other ways. The large lakes created by dams can displace millions of people and animals and drown plants. Smaller hydro machines placed in streams are looking like a better choice in the years ahead.

Not all of Earth's water sloshes around on its surface. The planet also holds water underground, where Earth's natural heat warms it up. The planet's hot, rocky guts give off 100 *billion* times more

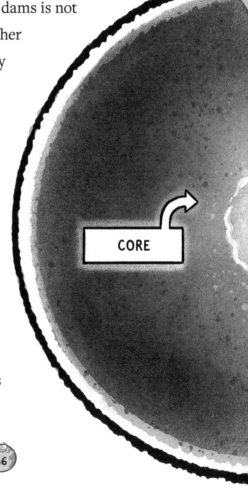

CORE

energy than the whole world uses today. People can and do use that steamy water, that geothermal heat, to drive turbines in power plants. The country of Kenya gets half its electricity from geothermal heat. Iceland gets a third. And even households can draw on warm underground waters with their own backyard geothermal wells. Geothermal energy can be expensive to set up at first, but it can save us and the planet a lot of pain and money in the long run.

You might need to explain to your grown-ups that some energy solutions are good for the long run, and some are more short-term. Take biomass, which is mostly easily grown plants and their leftovers. It includes weedy plants such as switchgrass and the bits and pieces of wood left behind when trees are cut down. We harvest the weedy plants, they grow back, and meanwhile we burn the biomass, this plant trash, to make energy.

"But wait," say your adults.

"Doesn't this send carbon into the air? I thought we weren't supposed to do that?"

It does give off carbon, but the newly grown plants that replace the old ones take the carbon back out again. This is known as a "carbon-neutral" solution: It doesn't add greenhouse gases, but it doesn't remove any, either. Burning biomass isn't ideal, but when it's done right, it could be a bridge to carry us from our fossil fuel present to our renewable future.

What's for Lunch?

After all this talk about energy, your grown-ups might be getting tired and hungry. Perfect! It's the right time to talk to them about what and how they eat—because that has a surprisingly big effect on the climate too.

Half of all the land on Earth, aside from deserts and ice sheets, is used to grow our food. Most of it is used to raise and feed animals such as cows, sheep, and pigs. Those are good sources of healthful protein! your adults protest. Maybe, you'll say, but animals use an enormous amount of energy and resources. They need almost 100 times more land, per protein produced, than plants such as soybeans. (And remind your adults about the cow belch problem discussed on page 27.) Animals aside, almost all plant crops use fertilizers that contain nitrogen. Little microbes in the soil take in this nitrogen and give off nitrous oxide, a powerful greenhouse gas. Once it's grown, our food is then moved from place to place in trucks or ships, processed, packaged, refrigerated, and trucked again to stores. Picture greenhouse gases wafting into the air the whole time.

Then what happens? We throw it away. A lot of it, anyway. A third of the food we produce doesn't even make it into our mouths. Some spoils before it gets to the store.

MAMMALS, BY BIOMASS

Over the centuries, humans and their farmed mammals have spread across the planet. "Biomass" in this chart means the actual physical weight of mammal bodies on Earth.

WILD MAMMALS
4% global mammal biomass

HUMANS
34% global mammal biomass

The animals we raise outweigh all other mammals on Earth. Growing animals for food means replacing green forests with farms, using toxic fertilizers, packing meat in plastics, and pumping carbon into the air.

KEY

or   or   =

1 million metric tons of carbon
(2015 data)

LIVESTOCK AND PETS
62% global mammal biomass

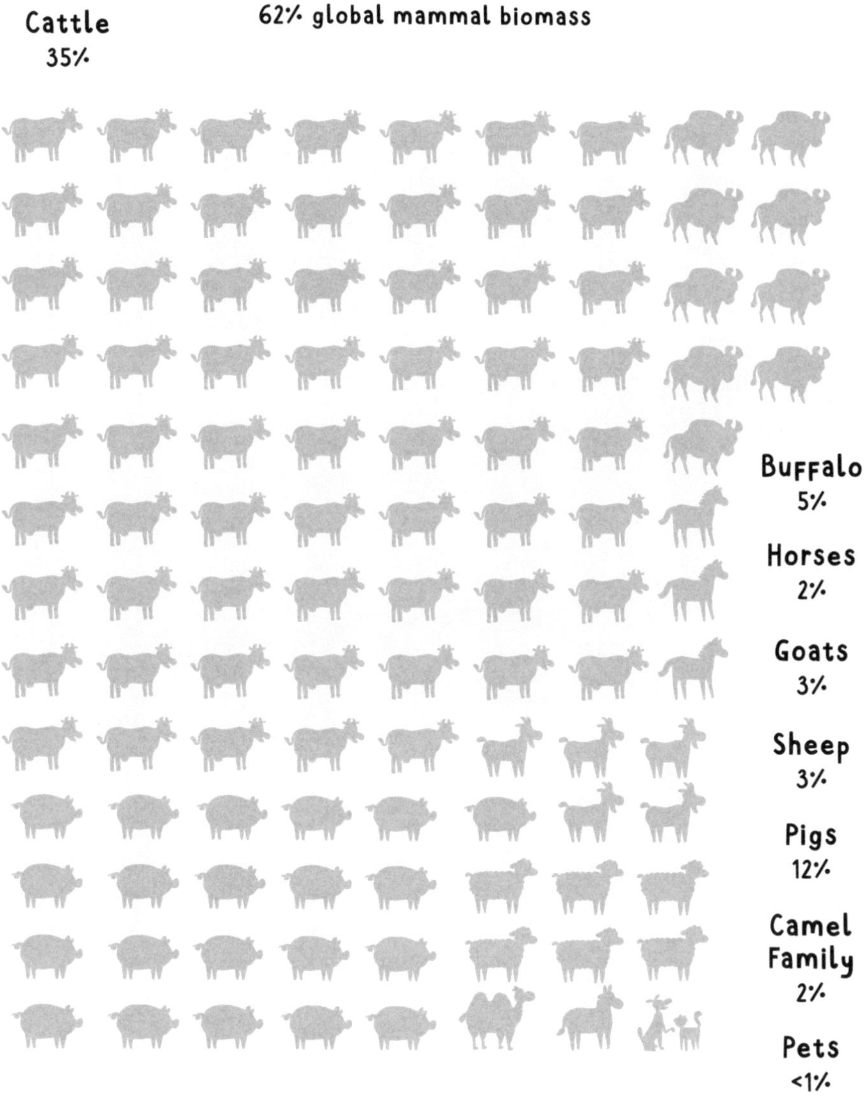

Cattle
35%

Buffalo
5%

Horses
2%

Goats
3%

Sheep
3%

Pigs
12%

Camel Family
2%

Pets
<1%

Credit: Our World in Data

WHAT YOU CAN DO

Compost your food scraps. If you have a yard (or even space under your sink), you can set up a compost bin. Throw in nonmeat bits and pieces, such as eggshells, coffee grounds, and potato peels. Over the weeks, it will rot into great soil for your garden or houseplants.

Some is rejected because it looks funny—no lumpy potatoes for us! Some just doesn't get used in time and is dropped in the garbage can because we think the "sell by" date on the package means we have to toss it. In many places, most unused food ends up in landfills (big outdoor waste dumps). There, it gives off methane, which as we remember from our cow burps is a strong greenhouse gas.

This is one area where we all can make a difference right now. If we stop buying so much meat, especially from big animals such as cows and sheep, then the farmers of the world will stop raising so many carbon-powered animals. Land once used for growing animal feed could go back to trees and shrubs and butterflies. We could stop billions of tons of greenhouse gases from entering the air.

Your grown-ups can join millions of others in turning to a plant-rich diet. Some families already have "Meatless Mondays." Some people are VB6—vegan before 6 p.m. Others decide to go all the way vegetarian or vegan. It's up to you.

Your adults can also cut down on food waste at home. Help them plan their meals to use every last bit. Buy that crooked carrot! Eat those leftovers. Learn the best ways to store food so it lasts longer.

But...but... you mean
we can never have
burgers again?

NOPE!

You don't have to give up meat if you don't
want to. The key is to be mindful of what you
eat. If your diet is heavy on meat, just eat it less often.
Eat more plants. That's all.

These may seem like little things, but if everyone
switched to a plant-rich, low-waste diet, we would take a giant
step toward conquering climate change.

When we clear land for food, usually that means cutting
down trees—beautiful trees that can capture a lot more
carbon than crops can. Immense regions of our planet's
forests, especially tropical forests such as those in the
Amazon, have been cleared for farms and cities. Often, people
simply burn the trees, which pumps carbon into the air. Many

governments and organizations are now looking at replanting forests. We need to do it in a healthy way, with a mix of trees that is right for the landscape and forest animals. And we need to work with the people who live in and around those forests. They're not cutting them down for fun.

IT'S A FACT!

In southern Brazil, people have replanted almost 3 million native trees in an area that is home to rare black lion tamarin monkeys. Now they can jump from tree to tree again.

Clean Green Cooling

As your adults have learned, carbon is a big part, but not the only part, of climate change. One of the most powerful greenhouse gases comes from chemicals called hydrofluorocarbons. We'll take it easy and just call them HFCs. Refrigerators and air conditioners use HFCs. Unfortunately, the chemicals leak into the air, especially when the appliances are trashed at the end of their lives.

That's bad, but here's some good news for a change. People from more than 170 countries got together and decided to get rid of HFCs. Yes, adults actually did a sensible thing! Most countries are going to phase out and replace HFCs with cleaner chemicals. By the time they are phased out, that will have the same effect as cutting two years' worth of world carbon emissions.

Yay, grown-ups!

IT'S A FACT!

Many countries are already turning things around, greenhouse gas-wise. Countries in the European Union dropped their emissions by almost one-third between 1990 and 2020. The United States cut its heat-trapping gases by about one-fifth between 2005 and 2020. We need to move faster and do more, but there's hope!

Looking Forward

Eating less meat and moving to renewable energy are ways we can fight climate change right now. But sometimes grown-ups can get excited about solutions that aren't solving anything yet. Take carbon "capture and burial," for instance.

This is not as cool as it sounds, you have to tell your adults. It's true that some companies are trying out serious, scientific ways of removing and storing carbon from the air. Often, this means using machines to separate carbon dioxide from other gases coming out of power plants. The carbon dioxide is pressed and turned into liquid. Then the companies stash it somewhere, often by burying it under the earth. Unfortunately, this effort still has a lot of problems. You can only bury carbon in certain kinds of rocks. You can only capture a small fraction of all the carbon given off by fossil fuels.

Plus, some of that captured carbon is then used by oil companies to help pull up more oil. It's worth studying, but so far, it just doesn't work well enough to solve our climate crisis.

How about bold, futuristic solutions like shooting clouds of particles into the atmosphere to cool Earth? We know that ash and gases like sulfur dioxide from volcanoes can act like a big grimy parasol to block sunlight. Why not try that ourselves by spraying sulfur into the air, the way volcanoes do?

Why not? Because we'd be messing with our entire planet. Some places might cool down, but others could heat up or dry up. Ice sheets might melt faster. And sulfur, when it falls into lakes and the ocean, makes them even more acidic. Meanwhile, carbon would still be building up under the clouds on our darker Earth.

Also—who decides who can experiment with Earth? Can one country decide that for the rest of us? One group of scientists? One kooky billionaire?

This kind of "geoengineering" is too new and too risky to use right now. Maybe in the years to come, scientists will work out a way to truly cool off the whole planet. But for now, you can tell your adults, we already know how to solve the climate crisis. We have to turn off the overflowing water.

Meanwhile... as we're fixing our climate problem, we're still living with our climate problem. Sea levels are rising now. Storms are getting stormier as we speak. We need to adapt to the effects we can't change.

And so we are. Coastal cities, such as Miami, Florida, are raising their street levels and improving how they handle

stormwater. In the country of Djibouti, people are planting mangrove forests along their shorelines. These twisty trees are natural barriers against floods. Island nations such as Kiribati are setting up weather stations that will warn them when big storms are blowing in. With water rising around their ankles and wildfires racing across their backyards, people are moving, building, and changing where they can.

Remind your grown-ups, though, that adapting to climate change is not the same as fixing climate change. Not by a long shot. Fix AND adapt—that's the key.

What if we can't adapt to climate change? Maybe then we could just move to Mars. Wouldn't that be fun?

NOPE!

Some people have suggested that we can all live on Mars if Earth gets too bad. No. Just... no. Even at its hottest, stormiest worst, Earth is a paradise compared to Mars. Mars has no breathable air. It has no food.

Its average temperature is minus 81°F (–63°C). We don't have even one spaceship, much less hundreds of thousands to carry humans on the dangerous journey to the red planet. A handful of superrich folks might want to hang out there someday. The rest of us will stay right here and solve our own problems.

WELCOME TO MARS!

Raise Your Voice

"We will not let you get away with this. Right here, right now is where we draw the line. The world is waking up. And change is coming, whether you like it or not."

Those bold words came from 16-year-old Greta Thunberg, talking to adults at a United Nations climate meeting. This Swedish activist is one of the world's best-known warriors against climate change. When she was 15, she started a movement now called Fridays for Future. Every Friday, she and other students would leave school to protest the lack of action on climate. That movement now has

millions of members around the world. Other young people in many countries now lead similar movements, such as the Sunrise Movement and Youth4Climate.

Kids are already working on this, you can tell your grown-ups. We understand that we'll be living with climate change for a long time. But the adults have to join us. They have the power to fix this right now. They can't just sit back and let the children take the heat.

It's honestly not that hard. We've talked about making simple changes in our own lives: eating less meat, driving cleaner cars, popping in LED bulbs. But we also need to follow Greta Thunberg's example: We need to raise our voices.

Raise them responsibly. Guide your grown-ups to help. One of the best things adults can do is just chat about climate change with friends and neighbors. People may not always pay attention to the news, but they're interested in what their friends have to say. Give your grown-ups some hints:

- Talk about something you have in common. How have you seen climate change in your daily life? How has it affected you and your friends personally? What have you done about it?

- Don't bother arguing with people who are flat-out climate deniers. There aren't that many of them, and they won't budge in their thinking.

- Don't be doom-y. That makes people give up. There's plenty we can do!

- Don't be a climate shamer. Don't wag your angry finger at folks who eat steaks or own gas-eating cars. You don't want to drive people away from the cause. There's room for different approaches in the climate fight. Also it's rude.

The other important way to raise your voice is to talk to the folks in power. You and your grown-ups can do that by telling politicians how important climate change is to you. Voters can elect people who will fight for a better climate. People can also vote with their money, by buying from companies that are working for a greener tomorrow.

Teach your grown-ups: It feels good to take action. No, it feels great. Grown-ups just have to listen to their kids. Together we can, genuinely, literally—no fooling— save the planet.

Test Your Grown-ups!

Now that you've taken your grown-ups through the basics of climate change, check to see if they were paying attention. It's quiz time!

1. What is the Goldilocks Zone?

    a) The area around the Sun where liquid water can exist
    b) The three bears' house
    c) A barbershop that cuts only blond hair
    d) The area around the Sun where everything is frozen solid

2. Which of the following is a greenhouse gas?

    a) Oxygen
    b) Carbon dioxide
    c) The smell from stinky cheese
    d) Nitrogen

3. What are fossil fuels made from?

    a) Triceratops bones
    b) Prehistoric trees and tiny prehistoric plants and animals
    c) Really thick water
    d) Mammoth hair

4. Pick one way scientists learn about our past climate.

a) They study cosmic rays.
b) They travel in a time machine.
c) They stare at clouds.
d) They study tree rings.

5. Which is the worst for the planet?

a) Cow burps
b) Cow farts
c) Human farts
d) Ladybug farts

6. How much have world temperatures risen since the Industrial Revolution?

a) 9°F (5°C)
b) 27°F (15°C)
c) Just over 1.8°F (1°C)
d) 0°F (0°C)

7. What is one good source of climate information?

a) Your dreams
b) A website called "I'm No Expert"
c) Your friend who learned everything from "I'm No Expert"
d) A well-respected scientific organization

8. Which of the following is *not* linked to climate change?

    a) Wildfires
    b) Rising seas
    c) Superstorms
    d) Bad dancing

9. Who in this list has the biggest carbon footprint?

    a) A fossil-fuel company
    b) An average person
    c) A hippopotamus
    d) A hippopotamus who stepped in carbon

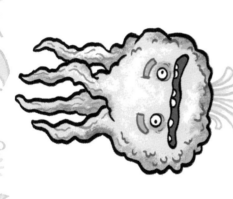
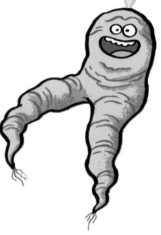

10. How much of the food we grow gets thrown away?

    a) None of it
    b) One-tenth
    c) One-third
    d) One-hundredth

11. How much higher will oceans be in the year 2050?

    a) One inch (2.5 cm)
    b) One foot (30 cm)
    c) One mile (1.6 km)
    d) Ten miles (16 km)

12. How tall are wind turbines?

   a) A little taller than me
   b) As tall as a giraffe
   c) As tall as a 20-story building
   d) Just tall enough to bump into a spaceship

13. Where would you *not* use a solar panel?

   a) In an open field
   b) On a rooftop
   c) In a desert
   d) In a dark basement in the middle of the night

14. Which one of the following activities gives off the *least* greenhouse gas?

   a) Building a highway from concrete
   b) Bicycling to work
   c) Raising cows with digestive problems
   d) Helicoptering to work

15. Which of these is a major way to fight climate change?

   a) Wishing everything would get better
   b) Pretending it's not happening
   c) Using renewable energy sources
   d) Deciding that someone else should deal with it

What You Can Do

Throughout this book, we've included tips on actions you and your grown-ups can take to help curb climate change. Below, we've listed a few more. You can do some of them at home, while others are aimed at your community, country—and world!

AT HOME

+ Cut down on food waste by writing the date when you bought or cooked your food on its package. Put the oldest items on the top shelf of your refrigerator, and use those first.

+ Save on household energy use by filling in heat-leaking cracks around windows and doors.

+ Buy food from local farmers markets. It uses less energy to reach you and is usually fresher.

+ Try out fun vegetarian or vegan recipes on Meatless Mondays and share them with family and friends.

+ When possible, use public transportation—buses, subways, or trains—instead of gas-powered cars to get around.

+ When you replace worn-out appliances, look for energy-saving machines. A typical new energy-efficient refrigerator, for example, uses half as much energy as an old one.

+ Stop buying bottled water—those plastic containers take a lot of energy to produce. Try reusable water bottles.

+ Turn off or unplug your electronics when you're not using them. Televisions, printers, game consoles, phone chargers, and other devices use a surprising amount of energy when they're idle.

IN YOUR COMMUNITY

+ Join a climate group—local, national, or international. See our Further Reading and Viewing page.

+ Keep climate in the news. Talk to your news outlets through social media or email. Tell them that climate coverage is important to you.

+ Talk to your elected officials. Email, call, or meet with them to let them know that climate is your top priority.

+ In cities, press your officials to green up neighborhoods with rooftop gardens, shade trees, and absorbent gardens. "Green infrastructure" not only cools things down, but it also absorbs the extra stormwater that comes with climate change.

+ Find out which companies have the best and worst effects on the world's climate (see, for instance, the Carbon Disclosure Project on the Sources page), and buy, or stop buying, from them.

Glossary

ATMOSPHERE—All of the gases around Earth or another planet or moon

BIOMASS—Plant and animal waste used for fuel

CARBON CAPTURE—The process of taking carbon dioxide given off by burning fuel and then storing it, so it doesn't enter the atmosphere

CARBON DIOXIDE—A greenhouse gas made of carbon and oxygen

CARBON FOOTPRINT—The total amount of carbon dioxide emissions from the actions of a person or group

CARBON NEUTRAL—Taking as much carbon out of the air as you are adding to the air

CLIMATE—The average weather of a place over many years

CLIMATE DENIER—A person who denies that human activities are causing changes in Earth's climate

COMPOST—A mix of decaying plants and other organic matter

DISINFORMATION—False information that is spread on purpose

DROUGHT—A long period of dry weather

ECHO CHAMBER—A place or a situation where a person hears only the opinions that reflect their own

ELECTRICAL GRID—The network of power lines and stations that sends electricity to houses and businesses

ENVIRONMENT—Everything that surrounds us on Earth, including all living things, the air, ocean, and land

FOSSIL FUEL—A fuel such as coal, oil, or natural gas that contains carbon and is made from the remains of ancient plants and animals

GEOENGINEERING—Making a big change in Earth's natural environment to fight climate change

GEOTHERMAL ENERGY—Energy that uses heat from inside Earth

GOLDILOCKS ZONE—The area around the Sun or other star that is neither too hot nor too cold for liquid water

GREENHOUSE GAS—A gas that traps heat in the atmosphere

HABITAT—The place where a plant or animal typically lives and grows

HYDROFLUOROCARBON (HFC)—A gas made of carbon, fluorine, and hydrogen; hydrofluorocarbons are powerful greenhouses gases

HYDROPOWER—Electricity made by machines powered by running water; also called hydroelectric power

INDUSTRIAL REVOLUTION—A time in history, beginning around 1760, when workers began to move from farming to making products in factories and cities

LANDFILL—An area where garbage is buried between layers of earth

METHANE—A powerful greenhouse gas made of carbon and hydrogen

MISINFORMATION—Incorrect information

NET-ZERO EMISSIONS—Removing the same amount of carbon from the air as goes into it

RECYCLE—To process something so it can be reused

RENEWABLE ENERGY—Energy that comes from natural sources, such as the wind or the sun, that don't run out

SATELLITE—An object, such as a moon or spacecraft, that orbits another body in space

SOLAR POWER—Renewable energy that is made by turning sunlight into electricity

TURBINE—An engine that turns the movement of air or water into energy

WEATHER—The state of the atmosphere (such as cold, hot, wet, or dry) in one place at one particular time

WIND TURBINE—A machine that turns the energy of the wind into electrical energy; sometimes called a windmill

Author's Sources

BOOKS

Emanuel, Kerry. *What We Know About Climate Change.* Cambridge, MA: MIT Press, 2018.

Hawken, Paul, ed. *Drawdown.* New York: Penguin Books, 2017.

Hayhoe, Katharine. *Saving Us.* New York: Simon & Schuster, 2021.

Mann, Michael, and Tom Toles. *The Madhouse Effect.* New York: Columbia University Press, 2016.

Mann, Michael. *The New Climate War.* New York: Public Affairs, 2021.

WEBSITES

Britannica Climate Change Facts: www.britannica.com/facts/climate-change

CarbonBrief: www.carbonbrief.org

Environmental Protection Agency Climate Change: www.epa.gov/climate-change

The Intergovernmental Panel on Climate Change: www.ipcc.ch

NASA Global Climate Change: climate.nasa.gov

National Centers for Environmental Information: www.ncei.noaa.gov

National Resources Defense Council: www.nrdc.org/demand-climate-action

Our World in Data: ourworldindata.org/explorers/climate-change

Project Drawdown: drawdown.org

UN Environment Programme: www.unep.org/about-un-environment

U.S. Department of Energy, Combating the Climate Crisis: www.energy.gov/combating-climate-crisis

Further Reading
and Viewing

BOOKS

FOR KIDS

Fleischman, Paul. *Eyes Wide Open.* Somerville, MA: Candlewick Press, 2014.

Gold, Hannah. *The Last Bear.* New York: HarperCollins, 2022.

Herbert, Megan, and Michael Mann. *The Tantrum That Saved the World.* Berkeley, CA: North Atlantic Books, 2022.

Jahren, Hope. *The Story of More* (Adapted for Young Adults). New York: Delacorte, 2021.

Kirby, Loll. *Old Enough to Save the Planet.* New York: Abrams, 2021.

Lloyd, Christopher. *It's Up to Us.* Maidstone: What on Earth Books, 2022.

Minoglio, Andrea. *Our World Out of Balance.* San Francisco: Blue Dot Kids Press, 2021.

FOR EVERYONE

Emanuel, Kerry. *What We Know About Climate Change*. Cambridge, MA: MIT Press, 2018.

Hawken, Paul, ed. *Drawdown*. New York: Penguin Books, 2017.

Hayhoe, Katharine. *Saving Us*. New York: Simon & Schuster, 2021.

Kolbert, Elizabeth. *Under a White Sky*. New York: Crown, 2021.

Mann, Michael. *The New Climate War*. New York: Public Affairs, 2021.

Thunberg, Greta. *No One Is Too Small to Make a Difference*. London: Penguin Books, 2019.

WEBSITES

FOR KIDS

American Museum of Natural History, Climate Change: www.amnh.org/explore/ology/climate-change

Britannica Kids, Climate: kids.britannica.com/kids/article/climate/352972

Fridays for Future: fridaysforfuture.org

Kids Fight Climate Change: www.kidsfightclimatechange.org

NASA Climate Kids: climatekids.nasa.gov

National Geographic Kids, Climate Change: kids.nationalgeographic.com/science/article/climate-change

Sunrise Movement: www.sunrisemovement.org

FOR EVERYONE

350.org: 350.org

Britannica Climate Change Facts: www.britannica.com/facts/climate-change

Carbon Disclosure Project (CDP): www.cdp.net/en/climate

Climate Feedback: climatefeedback.org

EPA Household Carbon Footprint Calculator: www.epa.gov/ghgemissions/household-carbon-footprint-calculator

Indigenous Environmental Network: www.ienearth.org

The Intergovernmental Panel on Climate Change: www.ipcc.ch

NASA Global Climate Change: climate.nasa.gov

National Centers for Environmental Information: www.ncei.noaa.gov

Our World in Data: ourworldindata.org/explorers/climate-change

The Planetary Health Diet: eatforum.org/eat-lancet-commission/the-planetary-health-diet-and-you

Project Drawdown: drawdown.org

Science Moms: sciencemoms.com

Skeptical Science: skepticalscience.com

Snopes Climate Change Denial, Debunked: www.snopes.com/collections/climate-change-denial-debunked

Tree Cities of the World: treecitiesoftheworld.org

UK Climate Risk: www.ukclimaterisk.org

United Nations Environment Programme: www.unep.org

Index

What on Earth Books is an imprint of What on Earth Publishing

The Black Barn, Wickhurst Farm, Leigh, Tonbridge, Kent, UK, TN11 8PS

30 Ridge Road Unit B, Greenbelt, Maryland, 20770, United States

First published in the United States in 2024

Foreword by Dr. Michael E. Mann

Written by Patricia Daniels

Fact-checking managed by Alison Eldridge

Fact-checking by Michele Metych

Illustrated by Aaron Blecha

Designed by Cara Llewellyn

Cover design by Andy Forshaw, Nell Wood and Daisy Symes

Developed by Potomac Global Media: Kevin Mulroy, Publisher;
Barbara Brownell Grogan, Editor in Chief;
Heather McElwain, Copyeditor and Proofreader

Index by Timothy Griffin

What on Earth Publishing: Nancy Feresten, Publisher and Editor-in-Chief;
Natalie Bellos, Editorial Director; Lucy Buxton, Editorial Assistant; Andy Forshaw, Art Director;
Daisy Symes, Senior Designer; Nell Wood, Designer; Lauren Fulbright, Production Director

Expert consultant: Dr. Michael E. Mann, Presidential Distinguished Professor and Director of the Center for Science, Sustainability, and the Media, University of Pennsylvania

Library of Congress Cataloging-in-Publication Data available upon request

ISBN: 9781804660317

LPP/Heshan, China/09/2023

1 3 5 7 9 10 8 6 4 2

whatonearthbooks.com